the seafood book

charmaine solomon

HAMLYN

First published in Great Britain
in 1998 by Hamlyn
an imprint of Reed International
Books Limited
Michelin House, 81 Fulham Road
London SW3 6RB
and Auckland, Melbourne,
Singapore and Toronto

Published 1997 by Hamlyn Australia
a part of Reed Books Australia
35 Cotham Rd, Kew
Victoria 3101
a division of Reed International
Books Australia Pty Limited

First published in 1993 by Hamlyn
Australia as part of Charmaine Solomon's
Asian Cooking Library

ISBN for UK edition 0 600 59468 8

A CIP catalogue for this book is available
from the British Library

National Library of Australia
cataloguing-in-publication data:

Solomon, Charmaine.
  The seafood book.
  Includes index.
  ISBN for Australian edition
  0 947334 72 6
  1. Cookery, (seafood).
  I. Title.

641.692

Designed by Guy Mirabella
Photographs by Michael Cook, Reg
Morrison and Rodney Weidland
Styling by Margaret Alcock
Food cooked by Nina Harris, Jill Pavey
China: Villeroy & Boch, Australia
Pty Ltd

Quark XPress by Melbourne
Media Services
Printed and bound in China by
Mandarin Book Production

A Metric/Imperial guide to Australian solid and liquid measures

Liquid Measures

Australian	Metric	Imperial
1 cup	250 ml	8 fl oz
1/2 cup	125 ml	4 fl oz
1/3 cup	75 ml	3 fl oz

Solid Measures

Australian	Metric	Imperial
1 cup	300 g	10 oz
1/2 cup	150 g	5 oz
1/3 cup	125 g	4 oz

Liquid Measures/Teaspoons/Tablespoons

A teaspoon holds approximately 5 ml in both
Australia and Britain. The British standard tablespoon
holds 15 ml, whilst the Australian holds 20 ml.

Australian	British
1 teaspoon	1 teaspoon
1 tablespoon	1 tablespoon
2 tablespoons	2 tablespoons
3 1/2 tablespoons	3 tablespoons
4 tablespoons	3 1/2 tablespoons

Notes

Convert cup measures to metric or
imperial measures where necessary.
Use one set of measurements only and
not a mixture. Standard level spoon
measurements are used in all recipes.
Eggs should be medium (size 3) unless
otherwise stated.
Milk should be full fat unless otherwise stated.
Pepper should be freshly milled unless
otherwise stated.
Fresh herbs should be used unless otherwise
stated. If unavailable use dried herbs as an
alternative but halve the quantities stated.

For ease of reference:
Capsicum = Pepper
Eggplant = Aubergine
Zucchini = Courgette

contents

soups

thai
hot sour prawn soup

serves 4

Prawn Stock (see p. 89)
2 stems lemon grass or 6 strips
   lemon rind
6 slices galangal
6 kaffir lime leaves
3 teaspoons chopped garlic
750 g (1½ lb) raw prawns, shelled
   and deveined

2 tablespoons fish sauce
2 tablespoons lime juice
¼ cup fresh coriander, chopped
3 fresh chillies, seeded and
   chopped

Make prawn stock, adding sliced lemon grass, galangal, lime leaves and garlic while it is simmering. Strain the stock. Reheat to boiling, add the prawns just until they turn pink and curl. Stir in fish sauce, lime juice, coriander and chillies and serve at once.

prawn and lentil soup

Make a meal of this South Indian soup with steamed rice.

serves 4

250 g (8 oz) green beans
150 g (4½ oz) red lentils
2 tablespoons oil
2 medium onions, finely sliced
1 clove garlic, finely chopped
1 teaspoon grated fresh ginger
2 fresh red chillies, split in half
  and seeded

1 teaspoon ground turmeric
500 g (1 lb) small prawns, shelled
  and deveined
salt to taste
125 ml (4 fl oz) canned coconut milk
  lemon juice to taste

Trim the beans, string if necessary, and cut in thin diagonal slices. Wash the lentils thoroughly; then drain. Heat the oil in a saucepan and fry the onion over a high heat, stirring constantly, until golden brown. Stir in the garlic and ginger, then add the chilli and turmeric; fry for a few seconds more. Add the lentils and fry, stirring, for about 2 minutes. Add 1 litre (32 fl oz) water and bring to the boil, stirring occasionally. Reduce the heat, cover and cook for 15 minutes. Add the prawns, beans and salt. Cook until the lentils are soft. Add the coconut milk mixed with 125 ml (4 fl oz) water. Stir in the lemon juice.

fish
and vermicelli soup

500 g (1 lb) John Dory, flathead,
  flounder or similar white fillets
2 teaspoons finely grated fresh
  ginger
3 tablespoons fish sauce
  salt to taste
¼ teaspoon ground black pepper
60 g (2 oz) bean thread vermicelli
1 tablespoon peanut oil
1 medium onion, sliced thinly

2 cloves garlic, crushed
4 curry leaves
1 teaspoon turmeric
½ teaspoon dried shrimp paste
2 teaspoons finely chopped lemon
  grass or 1 teaspoon grated
  lemon rind
  salt to taste
2 spring onions, finely sliced

With a sharp knife remove the skin and bones from the fish and coarsely chop the flesh. Place in a bowl and mix with ginger, 1 tablespoon of the fish sauce, salt and pepper. Leave to marinate. Cover the vermicelli in hot water and soak for 15 minutes. Heat the oil in a large saucepan and gently fry the onion, garlic and curry leaves, stirring frequently, until the onion is soft. Add the turmeric and dried shrimp paste and fry for 1 minute more, crushing the paste against side of the pan. Add the lemon grass or rind, drained vermicelli, remaining fish sauce, 1.5 litres (48 fl oz) hot water and salt to taste. Bring to the boil and cook for 5 minutes, then add the fish, reduce heat and simmer for 5 minutes. Remove from heat, pour into serving bowl and serve sprinkled with the spring onions.

sour
fish soup

This popular Penang dish has a delicious piquant flavour.

serves 4 to 6

1 kg (2 lb) jewfish or similar firm
   white fish including head
2 rounded tablespoons dried
   tamarind
6 large, dried red chillies
2 stems lemon grass
2 cm (¾ inch) slice fresh turmeric
   or 1 teaspoon ground
2 slices galangal in brine
2 brown onions, peeled and
   chopped roughly
1 teaspoon dried shrimp paste

2 tablespoons oil
2 teaspoons palm or brown sugar
1 teaspoon salt or to taste
750 g (1½ lb) fresh rice noodles or
   250 g (8 oz) dried
1 white onion, sliced thinly
6 slices half-ripe pineapple
1 small cucumber cut in strips
   fresh mint or Vietnamese mint
   leaves
   fresh basil leaves, optional

Clean and scale the fish and simmer in 750 ml (24 fl oz) water (lightly salted) for 15 minutes or until fish is cooked. Strain and reserve the stock. Discard the head. Flake half the fish and keep remaining half in large pieces, discarding the skin and bones.

Soak and dissolve the tamarind pulp in 750 ml (24 fl oz) hot water, strain through a nylon strainer and reserve. Break the stems off the chillies, shake out seeds and soak in 250 ml (8 fl oz) hot water for 10 minutes.

Slice the lemon grass finely, scrape the skin from turmeric and chop the galangal. Combine the lemon grass, turmeric and galangal with onions, soaked chillies and shrimp paste in blender or food processor. Add a little water to help blending, and process to a paste.

Heat the oil in a saucepan and fry the paste over a low heat, stirring, until cooked and fragrant, about 5 minutes. Add the tamarind liquid, bring to simmering point and cook for 5 minutes, then stir in sugar, salt, fish stock and flaked fish. Simmer for a further 10 minutes. Turn off the heat, add the larger pieces of fish and keep covered.

Pour some boiling water over fresh rice noodles in a colander (or cook dried rice noodles in boiling water for 3 minutes or until tender, drain well). Divide the noodles among individual bowls with sliced onion, pieces of pineapple and cucumber. Pour on the fish soup and sprinkle with the mint and basil leaves. Serve hot.

salads

seafood salad

To prevent seafood becoming tough and rubbery, it is imperative to avoid overcooking.

serves 4

375 g (12 oz) raw prawns
375 g (12 oz) cleaned squid
3 kaffir lime leaves, fresh or dried
3 sprigs fresh coriander
1 stem lemon grass, finely sliced
1 tablespoon fish sauce
3 tablespoons lime juice
1 teaspoon dark brown sugar

2 cloves garlic, crushed
2 teaspoons finely chopped ginger
freshly ground black pepper
4 spring onions, finely sliced,
including some green tops
⅓ cup lightly packed mint leaves
2 or 3 fresh red chillies, finely
sliced

Shell and devein the prawns (leaving tails on if you prefer). Slit and rinse the squid tubes. Wipe clean with kitchen paper if necessary. With a sharp knife, score the inside surface diagonally with narrow parallel lines, holding the knife at an angle of 45 degrees to make cuts without going right through. Cut the scored squid into bite-sized pieces.

Boil 750 ml (24 fl oz) water in a small saucepan with lime leaves, coriander and lemon grass for 5 minutes. Drop in the squid and immediately the pieces curl and turn opaque, remove with a slotted spoon. This should take less than 1 minute. Bring liquid back to boil and cook prawns, until they just turn pink. Lift out immediately with slotted spoon.

In a serving bowl mix fish sauce, lime juice, sugar, garlic, ginger and pepper. Toss seafood in the dressing, then add the spring onions, mint and chillies, and toss lightly.

thai
hot and sour prawn salad

500 g (1 lb) medium-sized raw prawns
2 slices fresh or brined galangal
2 strips finely peeled lemon rind
1 stem lemon grass or finely grated
   rind of 1 lemon
1 clove garlic
½ teaspoon salt
2 tablespoons white vinegar
2 tablespoons fish sauce
1 tablespoon lemon juice
2 teaspoons palm or brown sugar

2 fresh red chillies, finely sliced
1 fresh Thai lime leaf, cut into
   thread-like slivers
2 small seedless cucumbers,
   sliced
1 red capsicum, diced
1 small purple (Spanish) onion,
   sliced
⅓ cup roughly chopped fresh
   coriander leaves
lettuce for garnish

Shell and devein the prawns, leaving the tails on. Wash and drain. In a wok, bring to the boil 500 ml (16 fl oz) of water with the galangal and lemon rind. Add prawns and cook until they just start to curl. Remove with a slotted spoon and drain.

Peel the outer layers off the lemon grass and finely slice the tender white portion. Crush the garlic with salt. In a bowl mix the vinegar, fish sauce, lemon juice, sugar, chillies and garlic together. Add the remaining ingredients, except the lettuce, and toss to coat with dressing. Allow to stand 15 minutes for the flavours to develop. Serve surrounded with lettuce as part of a Thai meal.

crayfish
and coconut salad

serves 4

1 large or 2 medium-sized cooked
  crayfish
2 teaspoons sugar
180 ml (6 fl oz) fresh lime juice
2 small purple onions, sliced finely
6 red chillies, seeded and sliced
2 teaspoons rice flour
400 ml (13 fl oz) canned coconut milk
2 tablespoons fish sauce
4 fresh kaffir lime leaves, shredded

With a sharp knife cut into the crayfish from underneath, removing the meat from tail. Cut across into rounds. Reserve claws and legs. Place crayfish rounds in a bowl. Stir the sugar into the lime juice until dissolved, then pour over crayfish. Add a few slices of onion and half the chillies. Gently mix and set aside.

Mix the rice flour with 2 tablespoons coconut milk. Heat the remaining coconut milk in a small saucepan. Stir in the rice flour mixture and cook until slightly thickened. Pour into a bowl to cool. Drain liquid from the crayfish and stir into the coconut milk; add the fish sauce. Pour the coconut milk dressing over the base of a serving dish. Arrange the crayfish slices on top. Pile the remaining onion and chilli slices in the centre and garnish with kaffir lime leaves and crayfish claws and legs. Serve cold.

marinated fish salad

Variations on this method of 'cooking' fish abound throughout the Pacific. The acid in the lime or lemon juice turns the flesh opaque the same way that heat does. Choose a delicately flavoured fish.

serves 4

500 g (1 lb) white fish fillets
  lime or lemon juice
  salt to taste
1 purple onion, sliced very thinly
1 large, green capsicum, diced
3 spring onions, sliced finely
2 firm, red tomatoes, peeled and
  diced
125 ml (8 fl oz) canned coconut milk

1 small clove garlic, crushed
½ teaspoon finely grated fresh
  ginger
  salt and ground black pepper to
  taste
⅛ teaspoon ground turmeric
  lettuce leaves, washed
  chopped coriander leaves

Remove the skin and any bones from the fillets. Cut the fish into bite-sized pieces and put into a glass or ceramic bowl. Add sufficient strained lime juice to cover. Stir in the salt and onion with a wooden spoon (do not use metal utensils). Cover and refrigerate for at least 8 hours, stirring once or twice. Chill the prepared vegetables.

Mix the coconut milk, garlic, ginger, salt, pepper and turmeric. Drain the excess lime juice from the fish. Add the coconut dressing and mix well. Add the prepared vegetables, except for the lettuce. Toss and serve on a dish lined with lettuce leaves. Garnish with coriander leaves.

appetisers and entrées

1

crumbed
prawn cutlets

makes 12

12 large raw prawns
1 clove garlic
½ teaspoon salt
1 teaspoon finely grated fresh
 ginger
1 tablespoon light soy sauce
3 tablespoons plain flour
1 egg, beaten
 dry breadcrumbs or cornflake
 crumbs
750 ml (24 fl oz) peanut oil for deep-
 frying

Shell prawns, leaving only last segment and tail. Slit prawns along curve of back, taking care not to cut right through. Lift out sandy intestinal tract. Flatten prawns by pressing gently with heel of hand. Crush garlic to a smooth paste, adding salt. Mix garlic and ginger with soy sauce, brush over prawns and leave for 10 minutes.

Dip prawns in flour, then in beaten egg and finally into dry crumbs. Press gently to fix coating then place on a large plate in single layer and chill for 30 minutes.

Heat the oil in a wok and fry prawns, a few at a time, until golden brown. This should only take 1 or 2 minutes — do not overcook. Drain on paper towels and serve warm with a sweet chilli sauce or chilli mayonnaise.

prawn toast triangles

makes 24

6 slices sandwich bread
300 g (10 oz) large raw prawns,
   shelled and deveined
1 teaspoon finely grated fresh
   ginger

½ teaspoon salt or to taste
1 tablespoon beaten egg
2 teaspoons cornflour
   sprigs of basil or coriander
   oil for deep-frying

Trim crusts and air-dry bread on a wire rack for an hour. Finely chop the prawn meat. Combine with the ginger, salt, egg and cornflour, then spread on each slice of bread. With a sharp knife cut the slices diagonally into four. Press a basil leaf or sprig of coriander onto each triangle. Heat the oil and drop in a few pieces at a time, prawn side down. Fry until the bread is golden brown, then drain well on paper towels before serving.

grilled prawns

makes 12

12 large raw prawns
2 tablespoons light soy sauce
1 clove garlic, crushed

1 teaspoon finely grated ginger
   melted butter for brushing

Shell and devein the prawns, slit half way through, then press to flatten them. Mix the soy sauce, garlic and ginger and marinate the prawns for 15 minutes. Brush with melted butter and grill under a preheated griller until opaque. Do not overcook. Serve warm with a bowl of chilli mayonnaise for dipping.

fried

pork and crab rolls

These crisply deep-fried rolls would have to be one of the most popular items in Vietnamese cuisine. Go into any Vietnamese restaurant and you'll see, on every table, this favourite entrée being happily consumed by Orientals and Occidentals alike.

makes about 30

50 g bean starch noodles
meat from 1 cooked crab
300 g (10 oz) pork mince
3 spring onions, finely chopped
½ teaspoon salt
¼ teaspoon black pepper
2 tablespoons fish sauce
30 spring roll wrappers, 125-mm
(5-in) size

oil for frying
frilly Asian lettuce (or other
pliable lettuce)
sprigs of Vietnamese mint
(polygonum odoratum), fresh
coriander and mint
strips of cucumber

Soak the noodles in hot water for 15 minutes, drain and cut into short lengths with a sharp knife. Put in a bowl and combine with crab meat, pork mince, spring onions, salt, pepper and fish sauce. Mix well.

Thaw the spring roll pastry, carefully peel off individual sheets and put a scant tablespoon of filling close to one end. Roll up, turning in the ends so filling is enclosed. When all the rolls are made, heat the oil in a wok and deep-fry in batches so as not to crowd the pan or lower heat of oil too much. Lift out with a slotted spoon when golden brown and drain on paper towels.

Serve a plate of lettuce leaves and sprigs of pungent herbs with the rice paper rolls. Each person takes a roll, wraps it in a lettuce leaf and tucks in a sprig of mint, coriander or Vietnamese mint and a strip of cucumber. It is then dipped in the sauce (see below) and eaten.

Dipping Sauce

90 ml (3 fl oz) fish sauce
1 tablespoon vinegar
1 clove garlic
1 tablespoon sugar

2 teaspoons finely chopped
chillies or sambal oelek
juice and pulp of 1 lemon
1 tablespoon finely shredded
carrot, optional

Combine all the ingredients, except the carrots, with ¼ cup water, first crushing garlic to a smooth paste with some of the sugar. Cover and set aside. Before serving, stir in the carrot shreds and give each person a small individual bowl of sauce for dipping.

garlic scallops

serves 6

500 g (1 lb) scallops
1 tablespoon soy sauce
1 tablespoon oyster sauce
2 tablespoons dry sherry
1 teaspoon cornflour
3 teaspoons peanut oil
1 small red capsicum, finely sliced
3 large cloves garlic, finely
   chopped
1 teaspoon oriental sesame oil
shredded lettuce to garnish

Remove the dark vein from the scallops. Rinse and dry with paper towels. Mix the soy sauce, oyster sauce, dry sherry and cornflour in a small bowl.

Heat the wok, add the peanut oil and heat again for 30 seconds. Add the capsicum and stir-fry over a medium heat for 1 minute. Add the garlic and fry for a few seconds, stirring. Do not let the garlic brown or it will taste bitter. Add the scallops and stir-fry for 30 seconds. Pour in the sauce mixture. Stir until the sauce boils and thickens slightly; this will only take a few seconds. Remove from the heat, sprinkle sesame oil over the surface and mix. Serve immediately, garnished with shredded lettuce.

Note Do not overcook the scallops or they will shrink and become tough.

chilli prawn with lime

The lime leaves used in this recipe (as in most Thai recipes) are those of the kaffir lime. Its intense citrus fragrance is unique.

serves 4

500 g (1 lb) medium-sized raw
    prawns
2 teaspoons finely chopped fresh
    ginger
1 tablespoon fish sauce
2 teaspoons palm sugar or brown
    sugar
4 spring onions, sliced diagonally
4 fresh red chillies
2 teaspoons finely chopped fresh
    or frozen galangal
1 tablespoon chopped lemon
    grass

1 small onion, chopped finely
1 tablespoon Pepper and
    Coriander Paste (see p. 90)
2 tablespoons peanut oil
185 ml (6 fl oz) canned coconut milk
1 teaspoon rice flour
    salt to taste
    finely shredded fresh kaffir lime
    leaves (see Note) and fresh red
    chilli

Shell the prawns, but leave the tail segment intact. Carefully devein and using a sharp knife, slit each prawn in half from the top, for about a third of its length. Place in a bowl and mix in the ginger, fish sauce, sugar and spring onions. Marinate for 10 minutes.

Split the chillies and discard the seeds for less heat. Purée in a blender with the galangal, lemon grass, onion and pepper and coriander paste, scraping down the sides of the blender as necessary.

Heat the oil in a wok or frying pan, add the paste mixture and stir-fry until fragrant. Add the prawns with their marinade and cook until they change colour — about 3 minutes — turning constantly. Remove the pan from the heat.

Mix 2 tablespoons of the coconut milk with rice flour. Heat the remaining coconut milk in a small saucepan and, as it comes to the boil, stir in the rice flour mixture and continue stirring for a few seconds until it thickens. Add salt to taste and pour immediately into the centre of a serving plate or bowl. Place the prawns on the sauce and sprinkle with lime leaves and fresh chilli.

Note If fresh lime leaves are unavailable, use shreds of lime or lemon rind in preference to dried kaffir lime leaves.

squid with pork stuffing

6 dried shiitake (Chinese)
mushrooms
10 dried lily flowers (Golden
Needles)
½ cup bean thread vermicelli,
soaked
250 g (8 oz) minced pork
2 cloves garlic, crushed
1 teaspoon grated fresh ginger

3 spring onions, chopped finely
salt to taste
1 tablespoon fish sauce
¼ teaspoon ground black pepper
500 g (1 lb) medium-sized fresh
squid
3 tablespoons peanut oil for frying
shredded lettuce

Soak the mushrooms and lily flowers in hot water for 30 minutes. In a separate bowl soak

the vermicelli in hot water for 20 minutes. Discard the mushroom stems and any tough parts of

the flowers. Finely chop the remainder, place in a bowl and mix with the pork. Drain and chop the

vermicelli and add to the pork. Add the garlic, ginger, spring onions, salt, fish sauce and pepper to

the pork mixture and combine until well mixed.

Clean the squid thoroughly, discarding the head, beak and contents of the body. Reserve

the tentacles, chop finely and add to pork mixture. Wash the squid inside and out with cold, running

water, rubbing off the spotted skin. Pack the pork mixture into the squid and sew the opening shut with

a coarse needle and thread or fasten with wooden cocktail sticks.

Heat the oil in a wok or frying pan and sauté the squid over medium heat for 5 minutes.

Prick the surface of each squid with a fine skewer and continue frying for a further 10 minutes (or

longer if squid is large). When cooked and partly cooled, cut into slices and arrange on shredded

lettuce.

fish
or prawn cakes

Make these lightly seasoned seafood patties with fish in season or prawns, depending on availability and budget. Or mix both together.

serves 4

500 g (1 lb) firm white fish fillets, shelled raw prawns or a mixture of both
75 g (2½ oz) celery or water chestnuts, finely chopped
4 spring onions, finely shredded
1 teaspoon grated fresh ginger
salt to taste
white pepper to taste
2 tablespoons cornflour
2 tablespoons coriander leaves, chopped

3 eggs, lightly beaten
peanut oil for frying

Dipping Sauce

1 teaspoon sugar
2 tablespoons light soy sauce
1 tablespoon rice vinegar or white wine vinegar
1 teaspoon grated ginger

Carefully remove the skin and any bones from the fish fillets, or devein the prawns. Finely mince or chop the fish or prawn meat. Combine with the remaining ingredients, except the oil. Mix thoroughly.

Heat a heavy frying pan and add just enough oil to coat the base. Fry large spoonfuls of the mixture until golden, then turn to cook the other side. Remove from the pan and keep warm. Repeat with the remaining mixture, oiling the pan as necessary, until all the mixture is cooked. Serve warm with the dipping sauce.

To make the dipping sauce, stir all ingredients together in a small bowl until the sugar is dissolved.

spiced fish kebabs

You will need to buy fillets which can be cut into good-sized cubes for this dish. Firm-fleshed fish such as snapper, ling, jewfish and gemfish are ideal.

.serves 6

1 kg (2 lb) firm, white fish fillets
2 teaspoons grated fresh ginger
3 cloves garlic, crushed
   salt to taste
1 tablespoon ground coriander
1 teaspoon Garam Masala
   (see p. 89)
½ teaspoon chilli powder
1 tablespoon lemon juice
250 ml (8 fl oz) natural yoghurt
2 teaspoons plain (all-purpose)
   flour

Rinse the fillets and dry with a paper towel. Cut into 4-cm (1½-in) pieces. Place the remaining ingredients in a large bowl and mix well. Add the fish pieces and fold in gently until each piece is coated with marinade. Leave for 15 minutes at room temperature or longer in the refrigerator. Thread the fish on bamboo skewers, about four or five pieces on each, ensuring that the skin on each piece of fish is on one side of the skewer. (Soak skewers in water before use to prevent them burning under the griller.)

Place kebabs on an oiled tray under a pre-heated griller and cook 10 cm (4 in) away from heat with skin upwards for 4 minutes. Turn skewers and grill other side for 4 to 5 minutes, depending on the thickness of the fish. Be careful not to overcook. Serve immediately.

barbecued octopus

serves 4 to 6

1 kg (2 lb) small octopus
1 small clove garlic, crushed
1 teaspoon sugar
1 teaspoon finely grated fresh
   ginger
6 tablespoons Japanese soy sauce
6 tablespoons rice wine (mirin)
   vegetable oil for cooking
   lettuce and watercress

Clean the octopus by slitting open the head and removing the gut and beak and cutting out the eyes. Wash well and drain. You can leave tiny octopus whole or cut into pieces. Crush the garlic with the sugar and mix in a bowl with the ginger, soy sauce and mirin. Put the octopus in a bowl and toss with the marinade until all pieces are coated. Leave for 30 minutes. Remove the octopus from bowl, allowing any excess marinade to drain back, and grill over glowing coals or on a hot griddle plate, turning frequently until the flesh is just uniformly opaque. Be careful not to overcook as this toughens octopus.

Add 60 ml (2 fl oz) water to remaining marinade and quickly bring to the boil in a small saucepan. Serve octopus with marinade spooned over and accompanied by lettuce and watercress.

stuffed fried crab

serves 4

4 cooked blue swimmer crabs
250 g (8 oz) raw prawns, shelled and
  deveined
½ cup boiled bean thread
  vermicelli
125 g (4 oz) minced pork
2 tablespoons finely chopped
  spring onions
2 cloves garlic, crushed
salt to taste

ground black pepper to taste
2 tablespoons chopped coriander
  leaves
1 teaspoon finely chopped red
  chilli
1 tablespoon cornflour
1 egg, beaten
750 ml (24 fl oz) peanut oil for frying
  (more, if necessary)
coriander sprigs or chilli flowers

Carefully remove the top shell from the crabs, scrub away any patches
and dry the shells. Discard the grey, feathery gills and stomach bag. Crack
open the bodies and claws, remove meat and set aside. Chop the prawns
finely. Cut vermicelli into 2.5-cm (1-in) lengths. Put the crab meat,
prawns, vermicelli, pork and spring onions in a bowl.

Mix the garlic, salt, pepper, coriander and chilli into the beaten egg. Add
to the ingredients in the bowl and mix thoroughly. Fill the crab shells with
the mixture. Heat the oil in a wok or deep frying pan and fry the crabs,
ladling oil over top. Continue frying over a medium heat for about 7 or 8
minutes so that by the time mixture is golden brown on top, it is cooked
through. Drain on a paper towel, arrange on serving plate and garnish with
sprigs of coriander and chilli flowers.

fish
with crab sauce

serves 4

750 g (1½ lb) silver dory, John Dory
  or similar white fillets
1 teaspoon finely grated fresh
  ginger
salt to taste
2 tablespoons cornflour
oil for deep-frying

Crab Sauce

2 tablespoons peanut oil
6 spring onions, chopped
½ teaspoon finely grated fresh
  ginger
125 ml (4 fl oz) Fish Stock (see p. 89)
  or chicken stock
185 g (6 oz) crabmeat (see Note)
¼ teaspoon white pepper
2 teaspoons cornflour
salt to taste

Remove the skin from the fish using a sharp knife. Wash the fillets and dry with a paper towel. Place the fillets on a chopping board and rub with grated ginger. Cut in halves lengthwise and then into bite-sized pieces. Toss in a mixture of salt and cornflour.

Heat the oil in a wok or a small, deep frying pan and fry the fish, several pieces at a time, over medium heat for about 1 minute. As each batch is cooked, drain on a paper towel and keep warm while making sauce.

To make the Crab Sauce, heat the oil in a pan and fry the spring onions and ginger over a low heat for a few seconds, stirring constantly. Add stock, cover and simmer for a few minutes. Stir in the crabmeat and season to taste with pepper. Mix the cornflour with 1 tablespoon cold water until smooth, stir into the sauce and season with salt if necessary. Arrange the fish pieces on a dish, spoon sauce over and serve immediately.

Note It is now possible to buy packets of fresh crabmeat — a great improvement on the rather dry texture of canned crab. Ask your fish supplier.

prawn or crab omelette

serves 4

8 eggs
salt to taste
pinch black pepper
250 g (8 oz) cooked prawns
or 2 small or 1 large cooked
crab or 250 g (8 oz) frozen crab
meat, thawed
oil for frying
2 spring onions, chopped

Beat the eggs lightly and season with salt and pepper. Shell, devein and chop the prawns, or pick flesh from the crab. Heat 4 teaspoons oil in frying pan and sauté the spring onions for 1 minute. Mix with prawns or crab.

Heat 2 teaspoons of oil, pour in half of the beaten eggs and cook, drawing the egg mixture in from the sides of the pan until set on the bottom and creamy on top. Spoon half of the shellfish mixture down the centre of the omelette and fold the omelette over to enclose the filling. Transfer to a warm serving plate. Repeat with remaining beaten egg and filling. Serve with salad.

sashimi

A Japanese delicacy of raw fish that has become increasingly popular in other countries. The fish must be impeccably fresh, its delicate flavour contrasting beautifully with the accompaniments of hot green horseradish paste and soy sauce.

for each serving
125 g (4 oz) tuna, salmon, bream, bonito, kingfish, or jewfish
1 tablespoon finely shredded giant white radish (daikon)
1 tablespoon finely shredded carrot
1 sprig of watercress
1 teaspoon prepared green horseradish or wasabi (see Note)
Japanese soy sauce
rice wine (mirin) or dry sherry

You may find some fish — such as tuna — especially prepared for sashimi and available at fish markets, but apart from these you should not buy fillets or any frozen fish for this dish. Purchase the whole fish and have it filleted or fillet it yourself, removing all bones. Carefully cut away the skin.

With a sharp knife (and handling the fish as little as possible) cut fillet into thin slices and arrange on a serving plate. You can cut tuna and bonito in small cubes; other fish can be cut into bite-sized slices and overlapped; small fish and squid can be cut into thin strips. Part of the appeal is in the artistic arrangement of pieces.

Serve with shredded white radish and carrot and decorate with a sprig of watercress. Accompany each serving with a small mound of wasabi and an individual sauce dish holding Japanese soy sauce or a mixture of soy and mirin or sherry.

Note Wasabi is a pungent green powder available in tins. It is reconstituted (like dry mustard) by the addition of a little cold water. Go easy: it is every bit as hot as English mustard. Also sold in tubes as a paste.

steamed fish with noodles

serves 4 to 6

100 g (3½ oz) bean thread vermicelli
6 dried shiitake (Chinese)
  mushrooms
2 carrots
3 thin slices fresh ginger
1 large clove garlic
2 tablespoons fish sauce

750 g (1½ lb) firm white fish fillets
125 ml (4 fl oz) canned coconut milk
1 teaspoon rice flour
¼ teaspoon salt
  fresh coriander leaves
  finely sliced spring onions

Soak the noodles and mushrooms in separate bowls of hot water and cover for 30 minutes.

Simmer the mushrooms for 15 minutes, then cool, discard stems and slice the caps thinly. Drain the noodles and cut in short lengths. Peel the carrots and cut into matchstick strips. Cut the ginger into thin shreds and finely chop the garlic. Combine all these ingredients with fish sauce; place in a heatproof dish in a steamer, cover, and steam for 15 minutes. Arrange the fish fillets over the noodle mixture. Steam until the fish is opaque.

Heat the coconut milk in a small pan with the rice flour and the salt until thickened. Pour over the fish and serve garnished with coriander leaves and spring onion.

marinated fried fish

serves 4 to 6

750 g (1½ lb) fish fillets (snapper or
   bream)
2 medium onions
3 cloves garlic, roughly chopped
2 tablespoons chopped fresh
   ginger
1 fresh green chilli, seeded and
   chopped
1 medium ripe tomato, peeled and
   chopped
½ teaspoon ground black pepper
   salt to taste
½ teaspoon ground turmeric

2 tablespoons lime or lemon juice
60 g (2 oz) chick pea flour (besan)
   or plain flour
4 tablespoons sesame seeds
1 teaspoon paprika
1 egg, beaten
   oil for frying
1 tablespoon ghee
8 curry leaves
4 cardamom pods, bruised
1 small stick cinnamon
185 ml (6 fl oz) yoghurt

Skin the fish; wash and dry it, then cut into large serving pieces. Place in a single layer in a big dish. Roughly chop one onion and place in a blender or food processor with the garlic, ginger, chilli and tomato. Blend to a purée, then mix in pepper, salt, turmeric and lime or lemon juice. Pour the mixture over the fish, turning the pieces so that they are coated with marinade. Leave for 30 minutes. Finely slice the remaining onion and reserve.

Meanwhile mix the flour, sesame seeds, salt to taste and paprika. Scrape the marinade from the fish and reserve. Dip the fish pieces in beaten egg, then in the flour mixture, thoroughly coating the surface. Pour sufficient oil into a deep frying pan to cover base. Heat the oil and, when hot, fry a few pieces of fish at a time until golden brown. Remove with a slotted spoon and drain on a paper towel.

Pour off all but 1 tablespoon of oil from pan. Add the ghee and fry the curry leaves, cardamom, cinnamon and sliced onion, stirring until the onion is golden. Stir in the reserved marinade; fry until aromatic, then mix in the yoghurt. Simmer for 5 minutes. Spoon the sauce over the fish and serve with rice, chapatis or parathas.

steamed fish balls with sugar peas

serves 4

750 g (1½ lb) fillets of fish
1 teaspoon finely grated fresh
  ginger
2 cloves garlic, crushed
1 teaspoon salt or to taste
2 egg yolks
4 teaspoons cornflour

oriental sesame oil
2 tablespoons peanut oil
250 g (8 oz) sugar snap or snow
  peas, strings removed
250 ml (8 fl oz) Fish Stock (see p. 89)
  or chicken stock
2 tablespoons oyster sauce
1 teaspoon sugar

Remove the skin and any bones from the fish and chop very finely (a food processor is useful for this). Mix with the ginger, garlic, salt, egg yolk and 2 teaspoons of cornflour. Lightly grease your hands with some sesame oil and form the fish into small balls about 2.5 cm (1 in) across. Place balls on a plate; put plate on a rack and steam in a covered pan over gently boiling water for 10 minutes. Meanwhile mix the remaining cornflour with 1 tablespoon of cold water.

When the fish balls are cooked, heat the peanut oil in a wok and toss the sugar peas in oil until they turn bright green — about 1½ minutes. Push the peas to the side of the wok, pour in the stock, add the cornflour mixture and cook, stirring, until thickened and clear — about 1 minute. Stir in the oyster sauce and sugar; toss to coat the sugar peas.

Arrange the fish balls on a warm serving dish and spoon sugar peas and sauce over. Serve immediately.

trout
in piquant sauce

serves 4 to 6

1 ×1 kg (2 lb) rainbow trout
2 tablespoons cornflour
salt to taste
½ teaspoon five-spice powder
2 tablespoons dry sherry
2 tablespoons light soy sauce
2 teaspoons sugar
1 tablespoon rice vinegar or other
mild vinegar
1 teaspoon oriental sesame oil
250 ml (8 fl oz) peanut oil
2 spring onions, chopped
1 clove garlic, chopped finely
2 teaspoons finely chopped fresh
ginger
chopped coriander leaves

Wash and dry the fish and make deep, diagonal cuts on

both sides. Mix the cornflour, salt and five-spice powder.

Coat the trout with this mixture, rubbing it into the slashes.

Mix the sherry, soy sauce, sugar, vinegar and sesame oil with

125 ml (4 fl oz) water, stirring until the sugar dissolves.

Heat the oil in a wok and slide in the fish. Fry over a medium heat until

browned on one side (about 2 minutes), then turn over and fry the other side.

Remove the fish. Pour off all but 1 tablespoon of oil. Reheat and add the spring onions,

garlic and ginger; stir-fry for 1 minute without browning. Stir in the sherry mixture. Return

the fish and simmer, covered, over low heat for 5 minutes. Carefully turn the fish over and simmer

for a further 4 to 5 minutes. Transfer to a warmed serving dish and sprinkle with coriander leaves.

tandoori fish

This dish takes its name from the 'tandoor' or North Indian clay oven. As this oven reaches an intense heat, any fish cooked in it will be ready very quickly. You can still achieve a good result by cooking the fish over barbecue coals or under a preheated griller. The marinade traditionally used for tandoori fish gives it a distinctive red colour.

serves 4

1 × 1 kg (2 lb) bream, mullet, trevally, tailor or similar firm-fleshed fish
coarse sea salt
2 cloves garlic, crushed
2 teaspoons finely grated fresh ginger
1 teaspoon ground cummin
1 teaspoon ground coriander

1 teaspoon chilli powder
1 teaspoon ground turmeric
2 teaspoons paprika
salt to taste
lime or lemon juice
3 tablespoons melted ghee
2 teaspoons Garam Masala (see p. 89)

Buy the fish cleaned and scaled with the head removed. Clean the cavity of the fish by rubbing with damp paper towel dipped in salt. Wash the fish thoroughly under cold, running water then dry with a paper towel. Using a sharp knife, cut deep slashes along each side of the fish. In a bowl mix the garlic, ginger, cummin, coriander, chilli powder, turmeric and paprika with salt to taste and sufficient lime or lemon juice to make a thick paste. Rub the marinade over fish, inside the cavity and into the slashes.

Marinate for at least 1 hour in the refrigerator. Run a long metal skewer through fish from head to tail and grill, brushing with melted ghee. It should take 6 to 7 minutes on each side. When fish is almost ready, sprinkle with Garam Masala. Serve with an Indian bread such as naan or parathas.

fish fillets in hoi sin sauce

serves 4 to 6

750 g (1½ lb) bream, John Dory,
snapper or similar fresh white
fish fillets
4 tablespoons peanut oil
2 large cloves garlic, bruised
2 tablespoons light soy sauce
2 teaspoons finely grated fresh
ginger
2 teaspoons hoi sin sauce
shreds of spring onion for
garnish

With a sharp knife, remove the skin from the fish. Rinse the fillets and dry on paper towels.

Heat the oil in a wok and fry the garlic until golden, then remove and discard. Put the fillets into the

oil one at a time; turn each after a few seconds and move to the side of wok before adding the next.

When all the fish has been fried, sprinkle with soy sauce and ginger, cover and simmer for 1 minute.

Remove the wok from the heat and stir the hoi sin sauce into the liquid. Arrange fish on a platter,

spoon the sauce over and garnish with spring onion shreds. Serve with steamed rice.

fried
fish with mushroom sauce

This dish should be served immediately the fish is cooked, so it is best to prepare the sauce ingredients first and simmer the sauce while the fish is frying.

serves 4 to 6

2 ×1 kg (2 lb) snapper, bream or
    similar white fish
flour, seasoned with salt to taste
oil for frying
fresh coriander sprigs

Mushroom Sauce

16 dried shiitake (Chinese)
    mushrooms
125 ml (4 fl oz) vinegar
8 tablespoons sugar
4 tablespoons soy sauce
2 tablespoons cornflour
4 tablespoons diagonally sliced
    spring onions
8 tablespoons shredded red
    ginger

Purchase the fish cleaned and scaled. Trim the fins and tail with kitchen scissors and scrub the cavity with a paper towel dipped in coarse salt. Rinse and dry thoroughly. Using a sharp knife make deep diagonal slashes on each side of fish, forming diamond shapes in the flesh.

Dip the fish in seasoned flour, dust off excess. Deep-fry in hot oil, turning to fry both sides until golden brown. Drain on absorbent paper.

Carefully transfer the fish to a serving dish, spoon the sauce over and serve immediately, garnished with sprigs of fresh coriander, if desired.

To make the Mushroom Sauce, soak the mushrooms in hot water for 30 minutes, drain, discard the stems and cut the caps into slices. Put the mushroom slices, vinegar, sugar and soy sauce in a small saucepan with 375 ml (12 fl oz) water. Bring to the boil and simmer for 15 minutes. Mix the cornflour with 2 tablespoons cold water, stir into the sauce. Add the spring onions and cook, stirring, over a medium heat until the sauce becomes clear and thick. Remove from the heat and stir in the shredded ginger.

steamed
red emperor with ham

Important in Chinese cuisine, this dish is traditionally cooked with an expensive or rare fish of delicate flavour — try large fillets of red emperor, barramundi or coral trout for example.

Serves 4 to 6

500 g (1 lb) skinless fillets
salt
½ teaspoon sugar
pinch white pepper
1 teaspoon oriental sesame oil
4 teaspoons cornflour
6 dried shiitake (Chinese)
  mushrooms

small leaves of Chinese cabbage
  (choy sum or bok choy)
125 g (4 oz) cooked ham,
  sliced thinly
185 ml (6 fl oz) Fish Stock (see p. 89)
  or chicken stock

Wash fish and cut into thin slices. Sprinkle with ½ teaspoon salt, sugar, pepper, ½ teaspoon of the sesame oil and 2 teaspoons of the cornflour and mix well. Chill for 30 minutes.

Cover mushrooms with very hot water and leave to soak for 30 minutes, then cut off stems and slice caps. Trim small leaves of Chinese cabbage and take as many curved tips as there are pieces of fish. Arrange on a lightly oiled, heatproof serving dish a leaf, a slice of fish, a slice of ham cut a little smaller than the fish, and a slice of mushroom.

Steam over boiling water for 8 minutes or until fish has become opaque. While fish steams, bring stock to the boil and stir in remaining 2 teaspoons cornflour mixed with a tablespoon of cold water. When sauce boils and thickens remove from heat and stir in remaining ½ teaspoon sesame oil. Season to taste with salt and white pepper. Pour over fish and serve immediately.

hot
prawn curry

Along the coast of South India are found some of the best seafood dishes it is possible to enjoy, and this is one of them. The heat of chillies is tempered by smooth coconut milk.

serves 6

1 kg (2 lb) large raw prawns
6 dried red chillies
2 medium onions, roughly
   chopped
3 cloves garlic, chopped
3 teaspoons chopped fresh ginger
4 tablespoons oil
2 sprigs fresh curry leaves
1 teaspoon ground turmeric

1 teaspoon ground coriander
1 teaspoon ground cummin
½ teaspoon ground fennel
2 teaspoons paprika
1½ teaspoons salt, or to taste
375 ml (12 fl oz) canned coconut
   milk
   juice of half a lime or lemon

Shell and devein the prawns. Snip the stems off the chillies and shake out the seeds, unless you prefer a very hot curry. Soak the chillies in hot water for 5 minutes. Drain. Purée the chillies, onion, garlic and ginger in a blender or food processor.

Heat the oil in a frying pan, add the curry leaves and fry for 2 minutes. Add the puréed mixture and fry, stirring constantly, for 5 minutes. Add the ground spices and fry for 1 minute, stirring. Add the prawns and cook, stirring constantly, until they change colour. Stir in the salt, coconut milk and 125 ml (4 fl oz) water and simmer uncovered for 10 to 15 minutes. Stir in the lime or lemon juice and serve with rice.

indian fish curry with coconut

serves 4

4 fish cutlets
  lemon juice
  salt
4 large dried red chillies
4 teaspoons desiccated coconut
2 teaspoons ground coriander
1 teaspoon ground cummin
2 cloves garlic, finely chopped

1 teaspoon finely chopped fresh
  ginger
2 teaspoons tamarind pulp
4 teaspoons ghee or oil
2 small onions, finely chopped
125 ml (4 fl oz) canned coconut milk
  salt to taste

Wash the fish, rub with lemon juice and salt; then set aside. Soak the chillies in hot water for 10 minutes. In a dry pan toast the coconut, stirring it constantly, until brown. Remove the coconut to a plate and toast the coriander and cummin in the same pan over low heat, stirring constantly, and taking care they do not burn. Remove the chillies from the water and place with the coconut, spices, garlic and ginger in a blender and blend to a smooth paste, adding a little water if necessary. Soak the tamarind in 150 ml (5 fl oz) hot water, squeeze to dissolve; strain.

Heat the ghee or oil in a heavy pan and fry the onion, stirring frequently, until soft. Add the blended mixture and fry over a medium heat, stirring until it darkens and smells aromatic. Add the coconut milk, salt and tamarind liquid. Bring slowly to a simmer, stirring to prevent mixture curdling. Add the fish and simmer gently, uncovered, until cooked. Serve with rice.

burmese

fish kofta curry

This is my family's favourite fish recipe, taught to me by my grandmother who lived most of her life in Burma. Boneless fillets (shark sold as flake) are excellent in this dish. They can also be used to advantage in other fish curries as they are firm and do not break up when cooked.

serves 6

1 kg (2 lb) jewfish, cod or similar
   white fillets
1½ teaspoons salt or to taste
   black pepper to taste
1 medium onion, chopped finely
1 large clove garlic, crushed
2 teaspoons finely grated fresh
   ginger
2 tablespoons lime or lemon juice
1 tablespoon finely chopped fresh
   dill
2 slices white bread, soaked in
   hot water and squeezed dry

Curry

2 tablespoons oriental sesame oil
2 tablespoons peanut oil
2 large onions, chopped finely
1 tablespoon chopped garlic
1 tablespoon finely chopped fresh
   ginger
1 teaspoon ground turmeric
½ teaspoon chilli powder
1 teaspoon paprika, optional
3 large ripe tomatoes, peeled and
   chopped
   salt to taste
1 teaspoon dried shrimp paste
2 tablespoons chopped fresh
   coriander leaves
2 tablespoons lime or lemon juice

Remove the skin from the fish with a sharp knife. Carefully remove the bones and mince the fish finely or chop in food processor. Place the minced fish in a large bowl and thoroughly mix in remaining ingredients. Form mixture into about 24 walnut-sized balls or koftas.

To make the curry, heat oils in a large saucepan and fry the onions, garlic and ginger over a gentle heat, stirring frequently, until soft and golden. Stir in the turmeric, then remove from the heat and add the chilli powder, paprika, tomatoes and salt. Wrap the dried shrimp paste in aluminium foil and cook under a hot griller for a few minutes on each side. Remove from the wrapping, dissolve in 1½ cups hot water and add to the pan. Cook the sauce until the tomatoes become soft and pulpy. The liquid must cover the fish koftas, so add a little more hot water if liquid reduces too much. Gently transfer the koftas to the sauce and simmer over a medium heat until cooked — about 20 minutes. Do not stir until the koftas are cooked and firm or they will break up. Instead, shake the pan gently from time to time to prevent them sticking. Stir in the chopped coriander and lime or lemon juice and cook 5 minutes more. Serve with white rice.

Variation When a more delicately flavoured dish is desired, try making fish koftas by steaming or poaching them instead of cooking them in the curry sauce. The liquid they are poached in can be thickened with a little cornflour or they can be simmered in coconut milk. Serve with steamed rice and a steamed vegetable.

piquant fish curry

An ideal treatment for those dark-fleshed, oily fish which need strong flavours rather than delicate seasoning.

serves 6

1 kg (2 lb) fish steaks or fillets
1 tablespoon dried tamarind
1 tablespoon vegetable oil
2 teaspoons black mustard seeds
½ teaspoon fenugreek seeds
1 large onion, finely chopped
1 tablespoon finely chopped garlic
1 tablespoon finely grated fresh
   ginger
1 teaspoon ground turmeric
2 teaspoons ground cummin
   salt to taste

Rinse and dry the fish on a paper towel. Cut into serving pieces and set aside. Soak the dried tamarind in 375 ml (12 fl oz) hot water for 5 minutes, squeeze to dissolve the pulp. Strain, discarding the seeds and fibre.

Heat oil in a heavy saucepan and fry the mustard seeds until they pop. Add the fenugreek seeds, onion, garlic, and ginger and fry over a low heat, stirring, until the onion is soft and golden. Add the turmeric and cummin and stir for 1 minute. Then add the salt and tamarind liquid. Bring to a boil, add the fish and simmer over a low heat until the fish is cooked.

squid curry

500 g (1 lb) fresh squid
1 medium onion, chopped finely
2 cloves garlic, crushed
1 teaspoon finely grated fresh
  ginger
salt to taste
1 teaspoon chilli powder
½ teaspoon dried shrimp paste

250 ml (8 fl oz) canned coconut milk
8 candlenuts or 4 brazil nuts,
  grated
1 stalk fresh lemon grass, sliced
  finely
1 teaspoon brown sugar
1 teaspoon instant tamarind

Clean the squid, removing and discarding the head and ink sac. Cut off the tentacles and reserve. Wash the squid thoroughly inside and out, then rub any spotted skin from body. Slice the squid lengthwise into halves. Cut into bite-sized pieces. Put the remaining ingredients, except the sugar and tamarind, in a saucepan. Add 250 ml (8 fl oz) water and bring to a simmer, stirring constantly. Simmer the mixture, uncovered, until thickened, stirring occasionally. Meanwhile dissolve the sugar and tamarind in 60 ml (2 fl oz) hot water. Add the squid pieces and tentacles to the saucepan and simmer for only a few minutes — any longer will toughen the squid. Stir in the sugar and tamarind mixture, adding more salt to taste as required. Serve hot with rice and vegetables.

mussels
or clams in red curry sauce

serves 4

1 kg (2 lb) fresh mussels or clams
185 ml (6 fl oz) canned coconut milk
2 tablespoons Red Curry Paste
(see p. 90)
2 kaffir lime leaves
1–2 tablespoons fish sauce
1 teaspoon brown sugar or palm
sugar
2 tablespoons lime juice
1 red chilli, sliced finely
2 spring onions, sliced diagonally

Scrub the mussels under cold water, removing the beards. Discard those with open shells.

If using clams, rinse. Place in a large saucepan and add 185 ml (6 fl oz) water. Cover and cook over a high heat, shaking the pan occasionally. The shells should open after a few minutes. Remove and discard the top shells and any that remain closed. Strain the cooking liquid through a fine sieve.

Heat 125 ml (4 fl oz) of the coconut milk in a saucepan until oil appears around edges, mix in the red curry paste and cook, stirring, until fragrant. Stir in remaining coconut milk, the reserved cooking liquid, lime leaves, fish sauce and sugar and stir until the mixture simmers. Simmer for 10 minutes, stirring frequently. Add the lime juice, red chilli and spring onions, and ladle over mussels or clams. Serve with rice.

fish head curry

Much prized in Singapore, this dish has its origins in India. The large pieces of flesh within the head are boneless and very sweet. Some say the lips and eyes are the best parts.

serves 4

1 large fish head (snapper, bream) about 1.5 kg (3 lb)
2 slender eggplants
6 tender okra
4 tablespoons peanut oil
½ teaspoon fenugreek seeds
1 teaspoon black mustard seeds
3 green chillies, halved
2 sprigs curry leaves (about 20 dried leaves)
1 large onion, chopped finely

2 teaspoons chopped garlic
2 tablespoons ground coriander
1 tablespoon ground cummin
2 teaspoons ground fennel
1 teaspoon ground turmeric
½ teaspoon white pepper
2 tablespoons tamarind pulp
2 tablespoons tomato paste
2 ripe tomatoes, quartered
250 ml (8 fl oz) canned coconut milk
salt to taste

Clean and scale the fish head. Cut the eggplants and okra in 5-cm (2-in) lengths. Heat the oil and fry the eggplant and okra for about 3 minutes, remove from oil. Add the fenugreek and mustard seeds, chillies and curry leaves, cook for 1 minute. Add the onion and garlic and fry until soft and golden. Add the ground spices and fry, stirring, until fragrant.

Soak the tamarind pulp in 500 ml (16 fl oz) hot water for 10 minutes, squeeze to dissolve, then strain. Add to the pan with the tomato paste and tomatoes, bring to boil, add the coconut milk and salt. Add the fish head and vegetables, and simmer until cooked but still holding their shape. Serve with steamed white rice.

thai
green curry of fish

serves 4

500 g (1 lb) jewfish, kingfish,
    Spanish mackerel or similar
    firm cutlets
375 ml (12 fl oz) canned coconut
    milk
3 tablespoons Green Curry Paste
    (see p. 90)
6 fresh, frozen or dried kaffir lime
    leaves

½ teaspoon salt or to taste
1 tablespoon fish sauce
2 green chillies, seeded and
    chopped
4 tablespoons finely chopped
    fresh basil leaves

Wash the fish and trim away any spines with kitchen scissors. Cut into serving pieces. Mix the coconut milk with an equal amount of water in a large pan. Stir in the curry paste and bring to the boil, stirring constantly. Add the fish, lime leaves, salt and fish sauce; reduce heat and simmer, uncovered, until fish is cooked through — about 15 minutes. Add the chillies and basil and simmer a few minutes longer.

fish
curry with tomato

A curry that is mildly spicy.

serves 4 to 6

750 g (1½ lb) fish fillets or steaks
2 tablespoons ghee or oil
2 medium onions, finely chopped
2 teaspoons crushed garlic
2 teaspoons fresh ginger, chopped
  or grated
2 teaspoons ground coriander
1 teaspoon ground cummin
1 teaspoon ground turmeric

2 large ripe tomatoes, chopped
  salt to taste
1 teaspoon sugar
1½ teaspoons Garam Masala
  (see p. 89)
  squeeze of lime or lemon juice
2 tablespoons roughly chopped
  fresh coriander or mint

Wash the fish and dry with paper towels. Cut into serving pieces. Heat the ghee or oil in a saucepan and fry the onion, garlic and ginger over a low heat, stirring constantly, until onion is soft and golden. Add the coriander, cummin and turmeric and stir for a few minutes until the spices are cooked.

Add the tomato, salt, sugar and Garam Masala and cook, stirring, until reduced to a pulp. Add the fish to the pan, spooning the sauce over. Cover and simmer for 10 minutes, or until the fish turns opaque and flakes easily when pierced with knife. Remove from the heat, add the lime juice and chopped herbs and stir through. Serve with rice.

stir-fried scallops

As scallops are expensive, you can use a smaller amount and add a delicately flavoured vegetable.

serves 4

500 g (1 lb) fresh scallops
4 Chinese cabbages (choy sum) or
6 stems celery
4 tablespoons peanut oil
2 teaspoons finely grated fresh
ginger
8 spring onions, sliced finely
2 tablespoons dry sherry
4 teaspoons light soy sauce

Remove any dark streaks from the scallops. Cut the choy sum or celery into thin diagonal slices. Heat the oil in a wok and fry the ginger over a medium heat for 1 minute.

Add the scallops and stir-fry over a medium heat just until opaque — about 1 minute. Add the choy sum or celery and spring onions and toss for 1 minute more. Stir in the sherry and soy sauce until well mixed. Serve immediately with plain white rice.

stir-fried fish with mustard cabbage

serves 4

750 g (1½ lb) ling, barramundi,
  snapper or similar firm white
  fillets
1 small bunch mustard cabbage
  (gai choy)
2 tablespoons peanut oil
2 spring onions, chopped finely
2 small cloves garlic, crushed
1 teaspoon finely grated fresh
  ginger
2 tablespoons oyster sauce
2 tablespoons light soy sauce
2 teaspoons cornflour

Skin the fillets and cut into bite-sized pieces. Cut the mustard cabbage into thick diagonal slices, separating the leafy parts from the stems. Heat the peanut oil in a wok and fry the spring onion over a gentle heat just until soft. Add the garlic and ginger and stir for a few seconds, then increase the heat to medium and toss in the mustard cabbage stems. Stir-fry for 1 minute, then add the oyster and soy sauces with 125 ml (4 fl oz) hot water. Cover and simmer for 1 minute.

Add the fish pieces and leafy parts of the mustard cabbage and stir gently just until fish becomes opaque. Mix the cornflour with 2 tablespoons cold water and stir into the liquid. Bring the mixture to the boil, stirring until it thickens slightly. Serve immediately.

fish
with stir-fried vegetables

Serve with white rice and accompaniments such as bottled sambals.

serves 6

750 g (1½ lb) fish cutlets or steaks —
use a firm fish such as jewfish,
mackerel or tuna
salt
2 medium onions
3 large, fresh red chillies
1 red capsicum
185 g (6 oz) fresh green beans

1 cup sliced canned bamboo
shoots
3 cloves garlic, finely chopped
2 teaspoons finely grated fresh
ginger
2 tablespoons thick bean sauce
2 tablespoons peanut oil
1 tablespoon light soy sauce

Cut the fish into serving pieces. Sprinkle with salt and set aside. Peel and cut 1 onion in

six wedges lengthwise, then cut each section in half across and separate the layers. Remove the

membranes and seeds from the chillies and capsicum. Cut lengthwise into strips, then cut the strips

across in half. Trim the beans and slice diagonally. Slice the bamboo shoots to a similar size. Set each

vegetable aside separately.

Chop the remaining onion finely and mix with the garlic, ginger and bean sauce. Heat the

oil in a wok or frying pan and fry the onion mixture, stirring constantly, over medium heat until the

onion is soft. Add the green beans and stir-fry for 2 minutes. Add the chilli and capsicum strips with

the onion slices and stir-fry for 1 minute. Stir in the bamboo shoots with soy sauce and 125 ml

(4 fl oz) water. Dry fish on paper towels and add to pan. Bring to a simmer and cook, covered, until

fish is ready.

stir-fried squid with capsicums

serves 4

500 g (1 lb) large squid tubes
1 red and 1 green capsicum
3 tablespoons peanut oil
1 teaspoon finely grated fresh
    ginger
1 clove garlic, crushed
4 spring onions, sliced diagonally
1 teaspoon sugar
1 tablespoon light soy sauce
1 tablespoon dry sherry
2 teaspoons chilli sauce
1 teaspoon cornflour

Slit the squid tubes lengthwise and lightly score the inner surface, making a criss-cross pattern. Cut into pieces about 5 cm x 2.5 cm (2 in x 1 in). Cut the capsicums into bite-sized pieces.

Heat the oil in a wok, and stir-fry the squid over a high heat just until it curls — about 1 minute. Remove with a slotted spoon and drain on paper towel. Stir-fry the ginger, garlic, capsicum and spring onions for 1 minute, then add the sugar, soy sauce, sherry and chilli sauce. Mix the cornflour with 1 tablespoon water, add to the wok and stir until mixture thickens. Mix the squid into the sauce. Serve with steamed rice.

stir-fried prawns with vegetables and oyster sauce

Include your family's favourite vegetables in this dish. Consider Chinese cabbage, broccoli, spring onions, beans, baby corn, snow peas or sugar snap peas, mushrooms and carrots.

serves 4

500 g (1 lb) raw prawns
3 tablespoons peanut oil
1 teaspoon crushed garlic
½ teaspoon finely grated fresh
  ginger
3 cups vegetables, cut into bite-
  sized pieces
2 tablespoons oyster sauce
2 tablespoons dry sherry
2 teaspoons cornflour

Shell and devein the prawns. Heat 1 tablespoon of oil in a wok and stir-fry the vegetables until tender but still crunchy. Transfer to a dish.

Add the remaining oil to the wok and fry the garlic and ginger over a low heat, stirring constantly, until soft and golden. Add the prawns and stir-fry over a medium heat until they turn pink and curl. Add the oyster sauce, sherry, 125 ml (4 fl oz) water and bring to the boil. Mix the cornflour with 1 tablespoon cold water. Add to the liquid in the wok and cook, stirring, until the sauce thickens and clears. Return the vegetables and mix with the prawns and sauce until heated through. Do not overcook the prawns and vegetables. Serve immediately with hot white rice

spicy coconut mussels

serves 4

1 kg (2 lb) fresh mussels (see Note)
3 tablespoons ghee or oil
2 medium onions, chopped finely
4 cloves garlic, chopped finely
2 teaspoons finely chopped fresh ginger
3 fresh red chillies, seeded and chopped

½ teaspoon ground turmeric
1 tablespoon ground coriander
salt to taste
lime juice to taste
75 g (2½ oz) grated fresh coconut or 45 g (1½ oz) desiccated coconut, moistened with a little water
1 tablespoon chopped fresh coriander leaves

Scrub the mussels thoroughly under cold, running water and remove the beards. Discard any mussels that are not tightly closed. Heat the ghee in a large, deep saucepan and fry the onions, garlic and ginger over a medium heat, stirring frequently, until the onions are soft and golden. Add the chillies, turmeric and ground coriander and cook, stirring, for 3 minutes. Stir in the salt and 250 ml (8 fl oz) water, bring to the boil and simmer, covered, for 5 minutes. Add the mussels, cover and steam for a few minutes, transferring those that have opened to a serving dish. Continue cooking the remainder and discard any that refuse to open. Stir the lime juice into the sauce remaining in pan. Spoon the sauce over the mussels, sprinkle with coconut and coriander leaves and serve immediately with steamed white rice.

Note The instructions given are for live black mussels. Remember that mussels which are not tightly closed before cooking or do not open after cooking should be discarded. You can also used cooked mussels in this dish and simply make the spicy sauce and stir in the mussels until heated.

abalone
in oyster sauce

serves 4

4 dried shiitake (Chinese)
  mushrooms
1 × 450 g (1 lb) can abalone
24 snow peas
4 spring onions

Sauce

1 tablespoon oyster sauce
2 teaspoons light soy sauce
1 tablespoon dry sherry
2 teaspoons cornflour

Place the mushrooms in a small bowl and soak in hot water for 30 minutes, then discard the stalks and cut each mushroom into halves or quarters. Drain the abalone, reserving the liquid. Cut the abalone into paper-thin slices. Remove the strings from the snow peas. Cut the spring onions on the diagonal into bite-sized pieces.

To make the sauce, mix the oyster sauce, soy sauce and dry sherry in a bowl. Gradually add the cornflour, mixing until smooth. Stir in the liquid from the can. Pour into a saucepan and bring to the boil, stirring constantly. Add the mushrooms, snow peas and spring onions. Cook stirring constantly, until vegetables are tender but still crisp — about 2 minutes. Add the abalone and just heat it through. Be careful not to cook it over a high heat as it will become tough. Serve with steamed rice.

steamed

crayfish with ginger and black beans

A favourite at Chinese restaurants when price is no object. Australian restaurants usually serve crayfish or rock lobster rather than true lobster. Guard against overcooking or the flesh will be tough.

serves 4

2 live crayfish or uncooked lobster tails
2 teaspoons finely chopped garlic
2 teaspoons finely chopped ginger
4 teaspoons salted black beans, rinsed
2 tablespoons light soy sauce
2 tablespoons oriental sesame oil
4 spring onions, cut into fine shreds
2 tablespoons peanut oil

Drop the crayfish into boiling water for 1 minute or put into a freezer for 20 to 30 minutes to immobilise it. Chop the head from the body, cut the body in half lengthways and chop into sections. Put onto a heatproof plate, place in a steamer or on a trivet to hold it above the water level. Mix the garlic, ginger, black beans, soy sauce and sesame oil and pour over the crayfish. Cover and steam over boiling water for 10 minutes. Remove from the heat and sprinkle with shreds of spring onion. Heat the peanut oil until very hot and pour over crayfish so it sizzles. Serve at once.

velvet
prawns with asparagus tips

Two special techniques are illustrated here. One is to sprinkle prawns with salt and beat or whip them with chopsticks or a spoon. This makes them firm and crunchy. The other technique is called 'velveting', which means coating foods with egg white and cornflour.

serves 6

750 g (1½ lb) raw prawns
salt
1 egg white
1 tablespoon cornflour
1 tablespoon peanut oil
1 litre (2 pints) oil for deep-frying
1 clove garlic, crushed
2 teaspoons finely grated fresh ginger
250 g (8 oz) fresh asparagus tips

Sauce

125 ml (4 fl oz) Fish Stock (see p. 89)
or chicken stock
1 tablespoon oyster sauce
1 tablespoon dry sherry
1 teaspoon oriental sesame oil
2 teaspoons cornflour

Shell and devein the prawns, place in a large bowl, sprinkle with 1 teaspoon salt and stir vigorously for 1 minute. Transfer to a colander and rinse under cold running water for 1 minute, turning them with your hands. Drain and repeat this whole process of salting and rinsing twice more. Dry the prawns on paper towels, place in bowl, sprinkle with ½ teaspoon salt. Beat the egg white lightly and pour over the prawns. Sprinkle with the cornflour and mix well. Add 1 tablespoon oil, mix, cover and refrigerate for 1 hour.

Heat the wok and pour in 1 litre (2 pints) oil. When hot, but not too hot, add the prawns and stir so they don't stick together. As soon as they turn white pour through a metal sieve over a metal bowl. Wipe out the wok, heat again and return 1 tablespoon of the oil. Add the garlic and ginger, stir, then add the asparagus tips. Stir-fry over a high heat for 2 minutes.

Mix together all the sauce ingredients and pour into the wok. Stir until the mixture boils and thickens, then mix in the prawns and serve immediately with steamed rice.

singapore chilli crab

serves 4

2 medium-sized live crabs
4 tablespoons peanut oil
2 teaspoons finely chopped garlic
2 teaspoons finely chopped ginger
2 teaspoons chopped red chillies
60 ml (2 fl oz) tomato sauce
60 ml (2 fl oz) chilli sauce
1 tablespoon light soy sauce
½ teaspoon salt

Put the crabs in the freezer for 20 to 30 minutes to immobilise them.
Remove the top shell and feather-like tissue under it. Chop the bodies in two (four if they are large) and detach the large claws. Scrub any algae from shells. Crack the claws so the flavours can penetrate.

Heat the oil in a wok and fry the pieces of crab quickly, turning them until they become red. Remove from the wok and fry the garlic and ginger for a few seconds until aromatic. Add the chillies and remaining ingredients with 125 ml (4 fl oz) water. Return the pieces of crab to the pan and let them simmer in the sauce for 5 minutes. Serve with steamed white rice.

If using cooked crab, clean as described but only heat through in sauce — it is unnecessary to deep-fry. Reduce the oil to 1 tablespoon.

spiced seafood and rice

The preparation of this dish can be done a day ahead. It is then simply heated in the oven before serving. Garnish with cucumber and tomato slices or serve with a salad.

serves 6

1 kg (2 lb) firm white fish fillets
lemon juice
salt, pepper and ground
turmeric
500 g (1 lb) raw prawns
oil for frying
3 onions, finely chopped
3 cloves garlic, crushed
2 teaspoons finely grated fresh
ginger
1 tablespoon ground coriander
2 teaspoons ground cummin
1 large ripe tomato, peeled and
chopped
salt to taste
60 ml (2 fl oz) canned coconut milk

Spiced Rice

2 tablespoons ghee or oil
1 onion, finely sliced
1 quantity Whole Spice Mix (see
below)
500 g (1 lb) long grain rice
2 teaspoons salt or to taste

Whole Spice Mix

5 cardamom pods , bruised
4 whole cloves
1 × 8-cm (3-in) stick cinnamon

Wash the fish fillets and cut each into two or three pieces, removing any bones. Sprinkle lightly with lemon juice and salt, pepper and ground turmeric. Set aside for 15 minutes. Meanwhile shell and devein the prawns. Dry the fish on paper towels and fry in about 1.5 cm (½ in) of hot oil over a medium heat, turning carefully to lightly brown both sides. Remove the fish pieces as they are done.

Pour off the excess oil, leaving about 2 tablespoons in the pan. Fry the onions, garlic and ginger, stirring frequently, until the onion is soft and transparent. Add the coriander, cummin and ½ teaspoon of turmeric. Stir for 1 minute longer. Stir in the tomato, 125 ml (4 fl oz) water and salt to taste. Cover and simmer until tomato is soft and pulpy. Add the coconut milk and simmer, uncovered, until mixture is smooth and very thick. Add the fish and prawns, spooning the sauce over, and simmer for a few minutes more. Turn off the heat and leave while preparing the rice.

To make the spiced rice, heat all but a teaspoonful of ghee or oil and fry the sliced onion until golden. Add the Whole Spice Mix and rice and fry, stirring constantly, until rice is coated with ghee. Add 1 litre (2 pints) hot water and bring to the boil. Stir in salt to taste, turn heat very low, cover and cook for 15 minutes. Remove from heat and set aside, covered, for 5 minutes. Remove the whole spices.

Pre-heat the oven to 160°C (325°F). Grease a baking dish with the remaining teaspoon of ghee and spread a third of the Spiced Rice in one layer. On this spread a layer of fish mixture, another layer of rice, then remaining fish mixture and a top layer of rice. Cover and cook in oven for 25 minutes. Serve hot.

basics.

steamed white rice

This is the Chinese method for steaming rice. When cooked, the grains are well defined and separate but still cling together, which makes for easy eating with chopsticks.

serves 4 to 6

500 g (1 lb) short or medium grain rice
750 ml (24 fl oz) water

Wash the rice if necessary and drain well. Pour 750 ml (24 fl oz) water into a saucepan, add the rice and stir. Bring to the boil over a high heat and boil rapidly for 1 to 2 minutes. Reduce the heat to medium and continue cooking until holes appear in the rice and surface looks dimpled. Cover the pan with a tight-fitting lid (or place a layer of foil between the lid and pan), reduce the heat to minimum and continue cooking over very low heat for 10 minutes. Turn off the heat and leave the rice to sit undisturbed for a further 10 minutes. Do not remove the lid during this time.

Note Long grain rice is preferred for Indian dishes and gives a drier, more fluffy result. To cook 500 g (1 lb) long grain rice by this method, increase the amount of water to 875 ml (28 fl oz), as long grain rice has greater absorbency. At the end of cooking time fluff up the rice grains with a fork.

fish or prawn stock

**fish heads and trimmings or
prawn heads and shells
¼ teaspoon black peppercorns
3 slices fresh ginger
1 carrot, halved
2 stalks celery with leaves
1 large onion
2 stalks fresh coriander**

Wash the fish pieces or prawn heads and shells thoroughly. Put into a large saucepan and just cover with cold water. Add remaining ingredients and bring to the boil. Cover and simmer for 20 minutes if using fish, 30 minutes if using prawns. Strain the stock and use in soups or other seafood recipes.

garam masala

**makes about
½ cup**

**4 tablespoons coriander seeds
2 tablespoons cummin seeds
1 tablespoon whole black
   peppercorns
2 teaspoons cardamom seeds
   (measure after roasting and
   removing from pods)
4 ×7.5 cm (3 in) cinnamon sticks
1 teaspoon whole cloves
1 whole nutmeg**

Roast each spice separately in a small, heavy-based pan. Turn each onto a plate to cool as soon as it smells fragrant. Discard the pods from the roasted cardamom, using only seeds. Blend the spices except nutmeg to a fine powder. Finely grate the nutmeg and mix in. Store in an airtight container.

red curry paste

makes about 1 cup

10 large dried red chillies
2 small brown onions, chopped
1 teaspoon black peppercorns
2 teaspoons ground cummin
1 tablespoon ground coriander
2 tablespoons fresh coriander
   roots, chopped
1 teaspoon salt

1 stem lemon grass, sliced finely
   or 2 teaspoons lemon zest
2 slices galangal in brine
1 tablespoon chopped garlic
2 teaspoons dried shrimp paste
1 teaspoon turmeric
2 teaspoons paprika (see Note)

Remove the stems and seeds from the chillies and soak in just enough water to cover for

10 minutes. Purée in a blender with remaining ingredients. Store in a glass jar and refrigerate.

Note I have added paprika for the colour without too much heat.

green curry paste

makes about 1 cup

4 large or 8 small green chillies
1 medium onion, chopped
1 tablespoon chopped garlic
½ cup chopped fresh coriander,
   including roots, stems and
   leaves
¼ cup lemon grass, finely sliced, or
   thinly peeled zest of 1 lemon

1 tablespoon chopped galangal in
   brine
2 teaspoons ground coriander
1 teaspoon ground cummin
1 teaspoon black peppercorns
1 teaspoon ground turmeric
1 teaspoon dried shrimp paste

Blend and store as for Red Curry Paste.

pepper and coriander paste

makes about 1 cup

1 tablespoon chopped garlic
2 teaspoons of salt
2 tablespoons whole black
   peppercorns

2 cups coarsely chopped fresh
   coriander, including roots
2 tablespoons lemon juice

Crush garlic with salt to a smooth paste. Roast peppercorns in a dry pan for about

2 minutes. Finely chop the coriander roots, leaves and stems. Mix all the ingredients with lemon juice

and grind in a blender, adding a little water if necessary. Or use a mortar and pestle and pound to a

paste. May be stored in a glass jar in the refrigerator for 2 weeks if you add 1 teaspoon of citric acid

dissolved in a tablespoon or so of hot water.

Note Some of the ways I use this paste include marinating chicken fillets with a good thick coating

of it for 1 hour, then cooking them on the barbecue. Or, if I want a quick green chutney and don't have

any fresh herbs on hand, stir a spoonful of the paste into a cup of natural yoghurt. If you run out of

Thai Green Curry Paste never hesitate to use Pepper and Coriander Paste instead.

glossary

You can find most of these ingredients in Asian food stores, but many are sold in supermarkets.

Basmati rice
A fragrant rice with fine, long grains. Sold in Indian grocers and some supermarkets. Easy to cook but requires washing. Leave at least 30 minutes in colander to drain and dry.

Bean thread vermicelli
Made from mung beans, these noodles are fine and transparent.

Bird's eye chillies
Small, very hot chillies used in South-East Asian food.

Black beans
Salted, fermented soy beans are sold in packets or cans. Very salty, so rinse before use.

Bonito
A dark, oily fish with smooth, silver-grey skin.

Chillies
Fresh or dried chillies are an essential ingredient in Asian cooking. Wear gloves when handling them and don't touch your eyes or face with hands that might have even the slightest trace of chilli.

Chinese broccoli (gai larn)
A dark green vegetable with white flowers, used mostly for its stems.

Choy sum
One of the many green vegetables loosely called Chinese cabbage. Prized for its leaves and stems.

Coriander
The fresh herb and the dried seed are used in Asian cooking. When making Thai curry pastes look for fresh coriander with the roots intact.

Curry leaves
Increasingly available fresh, these leaves of murraya koenigii are essential in South Indian food. Instead of a sprig of fresh leaves, you can use about a dozen dried ones.

Fenugreek
Small, flat, pale brown seeds with a slightly bitter flavour, to use with discretion. An essential component of commercial curry powders.

Fish sauce
A thin, pale-coloured, very salty sauce made by salting fish and leaving to ferment. Very popular in the cuisines of South-East Asia.

Galangal, greater (laos, lengkuas and kha)
An aromatic rhizome, Alpinia galanga, similar in size and appearance to ginger but with different flavour. Sold in large slices bottled in brine. Keeps indefinitely in the refrigerator. Also sold as dried slices or powder.

Ginger
A very important rhizome in Asian seafood cookery, especially among the Chinese, who rely on ginger to remove the fishy taste.

Hoi sin sauce
A thick, sweet and spicy sauce used in Chinese dishes. Sold in jars, it keeps indefinitely without refrigeration.

Hot radish, bottled (chilli radish)
A good way to give zing to a dish. Use sparingly as it is pungent.

Kaffir lime leaves
Fragrant leaves of a special variety of citrus. These are worth searching for and in many capital cities they are sold fresh. Next best thing is frozen or dried leaves, although these are too tough to eat and can only be used in a soup or curry to impart flavour.

Laksa leaves (Vietnamese or Cambodian mint)
So-called in Singapore and Malaysia because the leaves are an integral part of the famous fish soup, Laksa. They are hot, adding wonderful flavour and are not mint at all, but polygonum odoratum. Ask for the plant by any of its names at good nurseries. It strikes easily in water and, if planted in a sunny spot and watered copiously, will grow in most temperate and tropical climates.

Lemon grass
A fragrant herb which can be simmered whole in a dish. When it is to be ground with other spices, however, it must first be thinly sliced as it is quite fibrous.

Lily buds
These exotic-sounding dried lily buds have little flavour, but I am assured that they have nutritional value.

Mushrooms, dried
The mushrooms used in this book are the variety known as shiitake and commonly called Chinese mushrooms, though they are common to Japanese and Korean food also. Do not substitute dried European mushrooms: the flavour is totally different.

Mustard cabbage (gai choy)
A tangy Chinese vegetable with bright green, ridged stems.

Okra
Slightly furry, green pods containing small, white seeds. Sweet and delicately flavoured, its most prominent feature is a mucilaginous texture which some people can't abide. Used in Cajun cooking to give texture to gumbo. Also very popular in Asian dishes.

Oriental sesame oil
Buy at Chinese groceries — the roasting of the sesame seeds give a wonderful flavour to the oil. Sesame oil sold at health food shops is pale and lacks this flavour.

Red ginger
Knobs of ginger preserved in a sweet and slightly salty deep red syrup. Finely sliced or shredded, they make a good addition to sauces for fish.

Rice wine (mirin)
Used in Japanese food. Substitute dry or sweet sherry.

Sambal ulek (oelek, olek)
Fresh chillies ground with salt and sold in jars. An easy way to get the flavour and heat of chillies.

Shrimp paste
Dried shrimp paste is a pungent ingredient used in small quantities in South-East Asian food. Sold in blocks or jars and lasting indefinitely, it brings out flavour in Asian food, much as anchovy sauce or anchovy paste does in Western food.

Wasabi (green horseradish)
A pungent root used in Japanese food. It has much the same effect as hot English mustard. Sold in powder or paste form, it is now not only found in Japanese shops, but almost every decent-sized fish market, as it is essential as a dip for sashimi or other raw fish dishes. No substitute.

White radish
Very large, shaped like a giant carrot, this is called daikon in Japanese and lo bok in Cantonese. Shredded and soaked in iced water, it becomes mild, sweet and crunchy.

index